Cavalcade Remembered-1925

Companion Volume to 'Cavalcade Reflections'
and 'Cavalcade Retrospect'

Published March 1976 by the Public Relations Department,
British Rail, Eastern Region, York

Text and captions set in 10 point Univers Light type,
1 point leaded, by ABM Typographics Ltd., Hull

Line and half-tone plates by Kings Town Engraving Co. Ltd.,
Hull

Printed by Galava Printing Company Ltd., Nelson

© Public Relations Department, British Rail,
Eastern Region, York

ISBN 0 7003 0033 3

Introduction
by Allan P. McLean

"At every lane-end immense numbers were collected," a diarist noted on 27 September 1825. The crowds had turned out to observe one of the most momentous occasions in the history of transport, although they probably did not realise the full significance of the event. Nor could they know that their awe and enthusiasm for the spectacle which marked the opening of the Stockton and Darlington Railway would be matched by other throngs of spectators 50, 100 and again 150 years later.

What was the significance of that day in 1825 when "Locomotion" coupled up to a train at Shildon and rumbled eastwards to Stockton? It was the start of a revolution, consolidating the development pioneered by earlier railways. The Stockton & Darlington brought together for the first time, all the elements that were to represent the railway system which developed during the rest of the nineteenth century—a public railway, operating a passenger and freight service and using steam locomotives. The success of the S. & D. helped prepare for the Liverpool & Manchester Railway—the first "Inter-City" route—which opened in 1830.

It was only right therefore that the cheers of the 1825 crowds should be echoed in that same corner of County Durham in 1875, 1925 and 1975. Each celebration, Jubilee, Centenary and Sesquicentenary,

Introduction continued

would bring vivid memories to succeeding generations.

When the North Eastern Railway, which had absorbed the pioneering S. & D. in 1863, celebrated the first 50 years in 1875 railways had become an essential part of the Victorian scene. Without the railways to move masses of people and raw materials and finished products Great Britain would never have become the workshop of the world. The celebrations could take place amid an air of assurance for a secure future. More development was still to come. The next great monuments of railway engineering were still to rise, notably the Forth Bridge, opened in 1890. Yearly passenger traffic of more than 500 million journeys and annual freight tonnage of almost 200 million were to rise to more than 1,275 million journeys and over 500 million tons by 1910.

It was a different picture by the 1920's with passenger journeys down from 1,579 million in 1920 to 1,232 million in 1925 and annual tonnage down from 318 million to 304 million between the same years. There was worse to come from the combined effects of road competition and industrial slump. By 1938 passenger traffic ebbed to 850 million journeys and goods fell to 265 million tons.

Any despondency was temporarily forgotten in the excitement of the centenary procession and exhibition although economic indicators for the fall from glory, leading to the General Strike of the following year, were already there. The Northern Echo of 3 July 1925, which reported the centenary parade, also reported a proposal to cut the pay of railway staff by five per cent because of financial difficulties. And there were stories on the same pages about "drastic proposals" to reduce miners' earnings, about pollution of the atmosphere, and about a speech made by Lloyd George in which he noted that unemployment was rising, shipping was laid up, steel blast furnaces were being damped down, there was a balance of trade deficit and the industrial situation was "very grave"

These pointers for concern may have a familiar ring to those who so recently turned out in 1975 to observe the Rail 150 Cavalcade. Also familiar to a modern ear would be sentiments expressed at a Centenary Banquet in the London & North Eastern Railway's Faverdale Works, Darlington, on 2 July 1925 by Sir Arthur Pease who called for sacrifice from workers and management to regain Britain's world trade. Sir Arthur also said that road and rail should co-operate. It was a great mistake for both road and rail to lose money by both trying to compete for the same traffic.

Viscount Grey of Falloden, who presided at the banquet, also had something to say of relevance to today when he stated that there was a feeling, not so much of congratulation about the past, as anxiety about the future as railways were passing through a difficult time and were unable to undertake many developments they wished to. But there was an expression of confidence from Lieut. Col. Wilfrid W. Ashley, M.P., Minister of Transport, who declared that Britain's railways were superior to any in the world—and that the "iron road" would always be supreme over road transport.

The railways industry was concerned for its future, faced by increasing road competition with the railway companies' hands tied behind their backs by a Parliament which insisted on published rates for goods being adhered to and unprofitable traffics being carried by train while the unfettered road competitors stepped

Introduction continued

in to pick and choose profitable business.

But the crowds turned out to celebrate in glorious sunshine. And the railway companies set out to give a good show. It was to be a magnificent display of confidence and prestige to put before the world a celebration of the merit and modernity of railways as a viable transport industry. The motor vehicle was beginning to gain the limelight before an admiring new generation. The centenary parade was the railways' answer to grab back their rightful place in the transport showroom window.

The centenary was 27 September 1925, but was marked in July because a meeting of the International Railway Congress was taking place then—so it was that on Wednesday 1 July the Royal Train steamed three minutes early into Darlington's Bank Top Station and the Earl of Durham welcomed the Duke and Duchess of York as they stepped on to the platform. Crowds waved and cheered as the Royal visitors travelled—by motor car—through flag-decked streets to Faverdale Wagon Works where more spectators stood at the gates "waiting on the tip-toes of expectancy", to quote the Northern Echo, whose John North Columnist of 50 years later still keeps up this worthy tradition of dipping a pen in the inkwells of inspiration. The Duke declared a major exhibition of locomotives and rolling stock open.

Next morning the Duke and Duchess—later to be King and Queen—arrived at Urlay Nook, between Stockton and Darlington, by train to take seats in a Grandstand to observe a parade of 53 locomotives and trains described by LNER publicity as "a unique and historic occasion which cannot recur". A quarter of a million attended. From early in the morning special trains had disgorged passengers from all over North East England. This was the culmination of months of detailed planning.

There were several activities to mark the celebrations, including the unveiling of a bronze plaque on a cottage which had once been a booking office of the Stockton & Darlington Railway, but the main excitement was the procession, counterpart of the 1975 Cavalcade. Examples of locomotives from 1822, to the modernity of 1925, were represented.

The parade came on to the route from two separate lines at North Shore Junction, Stockton, combining to run on the "wrong line" to Fighting Cocks, east of Darlington. Afterwards many exhibits continued to Faverdale Works. Final presentation was a replica of the first 1825 train hauled by "Locomotion" No. 1 of 1825, which could not be steamed but was powered by a concealed petrol motor.

The multitudes who watched in 1925 could not foresee the celebrations of 1975, to be enacted mainly as a salute to the steam locomotive which had surrendered its role as motive power by then to diesel and electric. Nor could they foresee the presence at that 150th anniversary of the 143 mph world-beating diesel High Speed Train forming the prototype of Inter-City for the late 1970's and 1980's . . .

RAILWAY BETWEEN STOCKTON AND DARLINGTON
SHOWING ROUTE OF PROCESSION

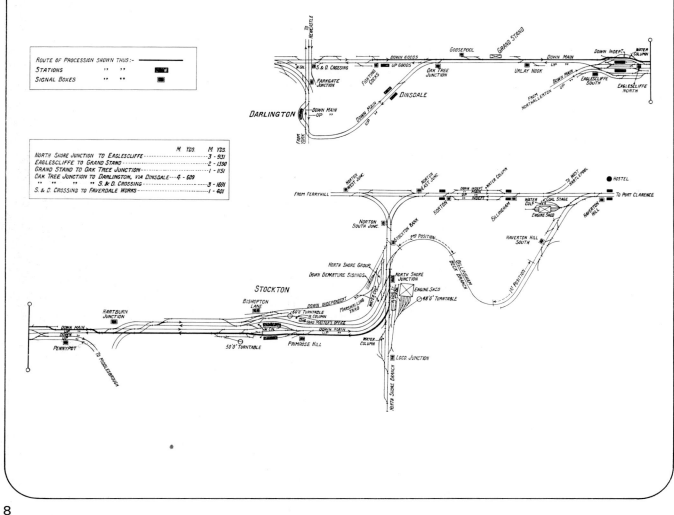

The Duke and Duchess of York (later King George VI and Queen Elizabeth) arrive at the Grandstand, having travelled by special train from Fencehouses, nearest station to Lambton Castle where they had stayed overnight as guests of the Earl of Durham.

They were met by L.N.E.R. Directors Viscount Grey of Falloden (to right of Duke) and Sir Hugh Bell (behind Duke) and the Company's Chief General Manager Sir Ralph Wedgwood (to left of Duchess).

Some 52 minutes earlier, at 9.45 a.m., the six-mile-long procession had begun to leave the Billingham Beck Branch at North Shore Junction. George Stephenson's Hetton Colliery Locomotive of 1822, with Driver Suddes at the controls, is shown here ready for the "off"—first exhibit in an event planned as a mobile demonstration of the way in which locomotive design evolved over 100 years.

Lady Bell, The Duke of York, Viscount Grey, The Duchess of York and Sir Hugh Bell, seated in the Grandstand, await the arrival of the procession.

In the foreground are silver models of "Locomotion" and the crude coach used by the Stockton and Darlington Railway Committee on opening day 1825. These mementos were presented to The Duke and Duchess by Viscount Grey at the end of the procession.

10.58 a.m., and the first exhibit, the Hetton Locomotive, passes the Grandstand at a stately six miles per hour. Although originally built in 1822 by George Stephenson and Nicholas Wood, the engine was rebuilt in 1857 and again in 1882, and so was able to move under its own power. The Hetton Locomotive spent several years in York Railway Museum but can now be seen at the Open Air Museum, Beamish.

Number Two in the procession, "Derwent" driven by George Danby of Shildon, at North Shore Junction. A typical Hackworth-type goods locomotive, "Derwent" was built by W. & A. Kitching of Darlington in 1845, and after several years of service on the Stockton & Darlington Railway, it was sold in 1869 to Pease & Partners for use on colliery lines.

"Derwent" trundling slowly past the Grandstand. In 1898, Pease & Partners presented "Derwent" to The North Eastern Railway, and after being restored it was placed on a plinth, with "Locomotion" at Bank Top Station. In 1975, "Derwent" moved yet again to a new home in The North Road Railway Museum at Darlington.

One of three locomotives representing The Scottish Constituent Companies of the L.N.E.R., this Class J31 0-6-0 goods locomotive was built for the North British Railway in 1867 to the design of William Wheatley. No. 381 (L.N.E.R. No. 10114) was withdrawn from service during 1925, given some superficial restoration and repainted in L.N.E.R. green but lettered N.B.R. on the tender. No. 381 was scrapped after the celebrations, but the last of the class survived until March 1937.

Another local favourite, No. 1275 was built in 1874 by Dübs and Co. of Glasgow, for use on the S. & D. section of the North Eastern Railway. The last survivor of the "long-boiler" type 0-6-0, No. 1275 was withdrawn from Malton shed in 1923, and carefully restored and repainted. After spending several years in York Railway Museum, No. 1275 went on loan to the new Darlington North Road Railway Museum in 1975.

No. 517 was one of 50 North Eastern Railway Class P2 (L.N.E.R. Class J26) 0-6-0 mineral locomotives built at Gateshead Works to the design of Wilson Worsdell during 1904/5. One of the last six survivors of the class, No. 517 was withdrawn from service as B.R. No. 65773 in June 1962. Spectators at the Grandstand enjoyed a musical accompaniment to the procession provided by the Harton Colliery Band.

One of 70 three-cylinder Express Goods locomotives built at Darlington North Road Works between 1919 and 1924, No. 934 belonged to N.E.R. Class S3 (L.N.E.R. Class B16). Running as number 6 in the procession No. 934 appeared in black livery lined out in red. The last locomotive in the class was withdrawn in 1961.

The Grouping of the railways in 1923 was to bring about many changes—and North Road Works were already experiencing some of these. This K3 class Express Goods locomotive No. 203 was one of 60 engines of basically Great Northern Railway design built at Darlington in 1924 and 1925. The class became extinct in 1962.

The first of six L.M.S. exhibits in the procession, No. 1881 was one of 170 four-cylinder compound mineral engines built between 1901 and 1904 by the London & North Western Railway, and designed by F. W. Webb. This compound design was not a great success and over the following years many of the class were re-built as two-cylinder simples, similar in appearance to the following exhibit.

The re-built simple version of the Webb 0-8-0 proved such rugged and efficient machines that new locomotives, similar to the re-builds, were constructed between 1910 and 1918. No. 9446 represents the final development, and was one of 60 locomotives built at Crewe in 1921 and 1922. The last members of the class were scrapped in 1964. As can be seen the route was lined with spectators and it was estimated that there were 200,000 people here at the Stockton end alone.

The Great Northern Railway equivalent of the L.N.W.R. heavy mineral locomotive was the three-cylinder 2-8-0 Class 02, designed by H. N. Gresley and introduced in 1918. Shown here on exhibition at Faverdale after the procession, No. 3501 was one of 26 built in 1923 and 1924 at Doncaster. No. 3461 of the same class was the first three-cylinder locomotive designed by Gresley.

The Great Western
Railway also
favoured the 2-8-0
wheel arrangement
for coal traffic, but
in 1919 produced a
variation in the
shape of No. 4700
shown here. The
"4700" class were
designated mixed
traffic locomotives
and were intended
to work Express
Goods and heavy
excursion trains.
The last four
locomotives in the
class were
withdrawn in 1964.

Projected as the freight counterpart of the Gresley Pacific, Class P1 2-8-2 No. 2393 was completed at Doncaster only a few days before the procession. The pony truck under the cab was fitted with a small booster steam engine to assist in starting 100 wagon coal trains. A further locomotive, No. 2394 was completed in November 1925, but the P1 Class was never really suited to contemporary operating conditions on the L.N.E.R. and both engines were scrapped in 1945.

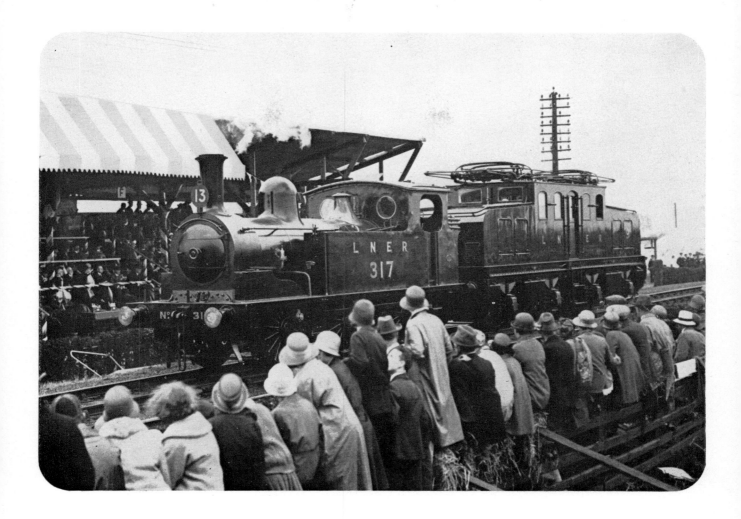

Electric Locomotive No. 9 was one of ten built at North Road Works in 1914 for use on the Shildon-Newport line. Working at 1,500 volts, four motors developing 275 B.H.P. each enabled the locos to haul 1,400 ton coal trains at a speed of 25 m.p.h. Electric working ceased in 1935, and the locomotives were stored, nine being scrapped in 1950, the tenth being used as a shunter at Ilford Carriage Sidings, before eventual scrapping in 1964.

The passenger locomotives were led by a replica of the broad gauge, G.W.R. "North Star" mounted on a wagon. The chimney was removed for the procession, or the locomotive would have been out of gauge. The original, built in 1837, worked until 1871, when it was preserved at Swindon. In 1906 the G.W.R. decided that the relic was in the way, and unforgiveably broke up "North Star" for scrap. The replica, constructed for the Centenary Celebrations, is now at Swindon Railway Museum.

At 8' 6" in diameter, the driving wheels of exhibit No. 15, "Cornwall" were said to be the largest on any surviving locomotive in the world. When originally built at Crewe for the L.N.W.R. in 1847 and as exhibited at The Great Exhibition of 1851, the boiler was actually mounted underneath the driving axle. "Cornwall" was rebuilt to its present form in 1858, and ran in ordinary service until 1902. The locomotive is at present stored at Crewe.

This 4-2-2 locomotive designed by Patrick Stirling for the Great Northern Railway and built in 1870, was the first of a series constructed at intervals up to 1895 for working East Coast Expresses. No. 1 was withdrawn from service in 1907 and apart from odd outings for exhibitions and publicity photographs was stored at King's Cross. This elegant locomotive can now be admired at The National Railway Museum, York.

The invention of steam sanding equipment in the late 1880s which helped to reduce wheel slip, led to a brief revival in the construction of single-driving wheel locomotives for express passenger work. Some companies, like the Midland Railway, had not built "singles" for twenty years or more. However, between 1887 and 1900, Derby Works built no less than 95 4-2-2 locomotives similar to No. 679 shown here. The last, No. 673, remained in service until 1928, and has been preserved.

In 1900, Gorton Works of the Great Central Railway produced six 4-2-2 locomotives for working expresses on their recently opened London extension. Although, with the increasing weight of trains, they were superseded by more powerful locomotives, all six survived into L.N.E.R. ownership. No. 5972, shown here at the Faverdale Exhibition, ran in the procession as Exhibit 18, and was the last of the class to be withdrawn from service in August 1927.

No. 910 was destined to be the only locomotive participating in the Stockton and Darlington Celebrations of 1875, 1925 and 1975. One of 55 similar locomotives built for the North Eastern Railway between 1872 and 1882, No. 910 worked for almost 50 years before being withdrawn from traffic in January 1925, and restored externally to original condition. After being towed in the 1975 Cavalcade, No. 910 returned to its permanent home in The National Railway Museum at York.

Ten years on, in 1885, the N.E.R. produced another 2-4-0 express passenger class of twenty locomotives, all of which survived to become L.N.E.R. Class E5. Nominally designed by a committee chaired by N.E.R. General Manager Henry Tennant, the Class were usually referred to as the ''Tennants'' and the first of the batch built at North Road, No. 1463 took part in the procession as Exhibit 20. On withdrawal from service in 1927, No. 1463 was restored, and is now at Darlington North Road Railway Museum.

The twenty locomotives of N.E.R. Class M built at Gateshead between 1892 and 1894 proved very speedy machines on the East Coast Expresses. A sister locomotive of No. 1620, which was item 21 in the procession, No. 1621 ran from Newcastle to Edinburgh in 119 minutes on 21 August 1895. No. 1620 was withdrawn in 1934, but 1621 lasted until 1945 and is now preserved in The National Railway Museum at York.

Named after the then Chairman of the Great Eastern Railway "Claud Hamilton" was built at Stratford in 1900 and appeared in the procession as rebuilt with Belpaire firebox early in 1925. "Claud Hamilton" was again rebuilt in 1937, and scrapped in 1947.

In 1898, No. 990—the first 4-4-2 tender locomotive to run in Britain emerged from the G.N.R. Works at Doncaster. The locomotive was named "Henry Oakley", after the recently retired G.N. General Manager, in 1900, and as L.N.E.R. No. 3990, ran as exhibit 23 in the procession. Unfortunately, the official photographer either failed to capture the engine, or spoilt the negative in processing, because this photograph is a fake! An 1898 view has been touched up with added procession running No. and figure 3 prefixes on cab-side and buffer beam.

In 1902, the Great Northern Railway produced an even larger 4-4-2 No. 251, which proved so successful that 93 similar engines were built between 1904 and 1910. The prototype ran in the procession as L.N.E.R. No. 3251 and together with "Henry Oakley" can be seen at The National Railway Museum, York.

Other railways soon began bringing out 4-4-2 designs, including the northern partners in the East Coast route, the North British and North Eastern Railways. L.N.E.R. Class C11 No. 9902 "Highland Chief" was one of a batch of six built for the North British Railway by Robert Stephenson & Co. in 1910. "Highland Chief" was withdrawn from traffic in 1936, but the last survivor, No. 9875 "Midlothian" was still running until mid-1939.

The North Eastern
Railway produced
their first 4-4-2 in
1903, and eventually
had a total of 72
in service to various
designs. These were
represented in the
procession by
No. 2207, a three-
cylinder simple of
Class Z1 (L.N.E.R.
Class C7) built at
North Road in 1917,
and withdrawn
from service in 1948.

The North Eastern Railway pioneered another express passenger locomotive type, the 4-6-0 of which 40 (Class S) were built between 1899 and 1909. Epitomising, as they did, the elegance which late Victorian locomotive design could achieve, it is hardly surprising that one of the class, No. 2006, should be awarded a Gold Medal at the Paris Exhibition of 1900. The locomotive carried replicas of the medal mounted in glass-fronted cases on the centre splashers.

The Great Central Railway also built both 4-4-2 and 4-6-0 types for Express Passenger working. Item 28 in the procession, L.N.E.R. Class B3 No. 6169, "Lord Faringdon" seen here at Faverdale, was built at the G.C.R. Works, Gorton in 1917. By the end of 1920, a further five similar locomotives had been completed. No. 6169 was named after the last G.C.R. Chairman, who became Deputy-Chairman of the L.N.E.R. and was actually among the Grandstand guests watching the procession.

London Midland and Scottish Railway No. 5900 "Sir Gilbert Claughton" was the first of 130 4-cylinder simple 4-6-0 locomotives constructed by the former London & North Western Railway between 1913 and 1921. They were the largest Express Passenger locomotives built by the L.N.W.R., but were regarded as lacking in boiler power and all were either rebuilt or scrapped by 1935.

The next logical development in size was the 4-6-2 and the Great Western Railway built a solitary locomotive of this type "The Great Bear" in 1908.

Next in the field was H. N. Gresley of the Great Northern, with two 4-6-2 engines completed in 1922 just before the grouping. A further 50 locos were built between 1923 and 1925, No. 2563 named after L.N.E.R. Chairman William Whitelaw, having been turned out by the North British Locomotive Co. of Glasgow in 1924.

There was no Exhibit 31, which should have been an experimental turbine locomotive developed by a private builder. Exhibit No. 32 was another electric locomotive, No. 13 built at North Road Works in 1922 for the North Eastern Railway's projected main line electrification between Newcastle and York. There were three pairs of motors of 300 h.p. each, in theory enabling 450 ton Express Passenger trains to run at up to 90 m.p.h. Unfortunately, the scheme was never carried out, and after several years in store No. 13 was scrapped in 1950.

The original "Aerolite" was built by Kitson Thompson & Hewitson of Leeds as a 2-2-2 well-tank in 1851 and appeared at the Great Exhibition of that year. It was purchased by the Leeds & Thirsk Railway, subsequently part of the N.E.R., and was nominally rebuilt in 1869, although the result was an entirely new locomotive. Further re-building followed in 1886, 1892 (as a two-cylinder compound 4-2-2T) and 1902 to its existing form. "Aerolite" is now in The National Railway Museum, York.

Exhibit No. 34, L.N.E.R. No. 6469 dated from 1873, and was built by Manning, Wardle & Co. of Leeds. The locomotive was purchased by the Manchester Sheffield and Lincolnshire (later Great Central) Railway from a civil engineering contractor in 1876. Apart from this brief moment of glory in the 1925 procession, No. 6469 spent its entire life shunting at Grimsby and Immingham Docks, and was scrapped in 1929.

"A roar of laughter greeted the appearance of what appeared to be a cross between a railway engine and a guards van . . ." reported the Northern Echo. In fact No. 7133 built 1897 was a locomotive of special type intended for use on railway lines at Docks or alongside public roads, where a conventional engine might startle horses. One of six locomotives built by the Great Eastern Railway, No. 7133 survived to become B.R. 68082.

Two 0-4-4 tank locomotives, Exhibit Nos. 36 and 37 represented successive generations of local passenger locomotives in the North East. No. 949, L.N.E.R. Class G6, built in 1874 was one of 124 similar engines known as the B.T.P. (Bogie Tank Passenger) class and was withdrawn in 1928. No. 1334 (L.N.E.R. Class G5) one of 110 built between 1894 and 1901 to designs by Wilson Worsdell was withdrawn in 1955. (Class J71 No. 1163 to rear of picture hauled electric loco No. 13 in the procession.)

The 45 Class D locomotives built by the N.E.R. at North Road in 1913/14 and 1920/22 were intended for short distance Express Passenger trains and were designated Class H1 by the L.N.E.R. All were rebuilt from the 4-4-4T wheel arrangement to the 4-6-2T type as Class A8 between 1931 and 1936.
No. 2151 ran as a 4-4-4T between 1913 and 1936 then as a 4-6-2T until 1960 when it was scrapped.

The re-building of Class H1 stemmed from the successful performance of the G.C.R. Class 9N 4-6-2T locomotives (L.N.E.R. Class A5). A total of 45 of these were built at intervals between 1911 and 1926. No. 5088, shown here starting out from North Shore Junction on the two-hour procession to Darlington, dated from 1923, and was withdrawn in 1958.

A tank engine version of the former Lancashire & Yorkshire Railway 4-6-0 which appeared later in the procession, L.M.S. No. 11112 was a four-cylinder simple of the 4-6-4 type. Only ten of the class were built all at Horwich in 1924, and, as they were non-standard engines, had comparatively short lives. No. 11112 was one of the first to be scrapped in 1938 and the rest had all gone by 1942.

The Great Western Railway made far more use of large tank locomotives for heavy freight work than any other Company. Ideally suited to the stiff gradients and short runs of the South Wales Coalfield, No. 5205 was a 2-8-0 tank locomotive built at Swindon in 1924, one of 175 similar engines, the design of which dated back to 1910. The last locomotive of this type was withdrawn in 1965.

Dwarfing all the previous exhibits, No. 2395 was the largest and most powerful locomotive ever to run in Britain. In effect two three-cylinder 2-8-0 locomotives articulated under a single chassis, the basic design was patented by Beyer Peacock of Manchester, who completed No. 2395 only a few days before the procession. The only example of this type to run on the L.N.E.R., No. 2395, was intended to assist heavy trains up inclines, and was scrapped in 1955.

Even in 1925, the use of internal combustion engines on rails was by no means new—the N.E.R. had been experimenting with various vehicles since 1903. No. 130Y, dating from 1922, was a standard Leyland road bus adapted to run on rails, and seems to have worked quite successfully in the Selby area until 1926, when someone carrying a naked flame paraffin lamp decided to check the level of petrol in the tank. The vehicle was destroyed in the ensuing conflagration.

No. 21057 was ordered by the N.E.R. but was not completed until that Company had become part of the L.N.E.R. Seating 40 passengers the car was powered by a 105 h.p. Daimler engine driving the single pair of wheels at the rear through a clutch and three-speed gear box. The car worked in the York and Hull areas until about 1934 when it was scrapped.

Steam was yet to have its final fling on branch line and light passenger service; Exhibit 45 showed the shape of things to come. The Sentinel Waggon Works in conjunction with Cammell Lairds began building steam powered railcars in 1923 and both the L.N.E.R. and L.M.S. purchased sample cars in 1925. The L.N.E.R. eventually had 85 Sentinels in service, but they were only moderately successful and were scrapped between 1939 and 1948.

It was fitting that the final section of the procession, the complete trains, should start with a reminder that railways had their roots in coal. Exhibit No. 46, hauled by former N.E.R. three-cylinder Class T3 0-8-0 No. 904, built in 1919, comprised a train of $10\frac{1}{2}$ ton, 20 ton and 40 ton "Self-Discharging" mineral wagons showing the gradual development of high capacity vehicles for coal and iron ore traffic. A total of 15 Class T3 (L.N.E.R. Q7) locomotives were built, and the class became extinct in 1962.

This view from the Grandstand, looking over the Press Enclosure, shows Exhibit 47, the Tableaux Train, hauled by No. 130, a former N.E.R. Class T1 0-8-0 built at Gateshead in 1902. Some 89 similar locomotives were built between 1901 and 1911, and 50 went on loan to France during the Great War. These had Chevron and Grenade symbols mounted on their cab sides to commemorate this spell "On Active Service". No. 130 was scrapped in 1950.

The following descriptions of the tableaux, which showed the evolution of the wheel in transport, are taken from a contemporary booklet published by the L.N.E.R. "The first tableau is allegorical. The symbolic wheel in the centre has, as supporters, on one side a group of early astrologers, and on the other modern engineering practice. The links of time join the two through the wheel."

"The second tableau depicts the first wheel. Early man, with flint and fire fells his tree, and transports this from the forest of tall straight trees to the stream on which he wishes to launch his dug-out canoe by using logs—the earliest wheels."

"In the third tableau, Royal Pharaohs, drawn by slaves on wheeled platforms, start the wheel in its manifold forms, and through the ages progress rolls on the wheels of chariot, wain and coach."

"For a brief space of time fashion discarded the wheel and beauty was borne under the eyes of gallants; coffee house patrons and tavern frequenters as here depicted."

"The wheel's story in transport opened its most famous chapter when Stephenson mounted an engine on wheels and steam locomotion was born. On one side, Stephenson, surrounded by a group of his friends and colliery smiths, explains the working of the model "Rocket" (sic)—on the other side, are modern mechanics handling modern materials and tools. From that little smithy grew the extensive engineering works at Darlington which have made the town famous in every corner of the globe."

The final tableau . . . "suggests the world-wide use of railways. From the few miles of permanent way which united Stockton and Darlington and over which the first train ran in 1825 have evolved the steel ribbons which today are traversed by millions of wheels, tying every corner of the Land to the Empire's Capital."

PRESS ONLY

Exhibit 48, a locomotive and train of carriages from the former Great North of Scotland Railway, showed travel in the 1860s. One of six Class K (L.N.E.R. D47/2) locomotives built by Nielson & Co. in 1866, engine No. 45 had been repainted in green G.N.S.R. livery for the procession, and after returning to Scotland, was officially withdrawn from service on 31 July 1925. The coaches never went home; they were purchased by the Harton Coal Company for use on their South Shields Marsden & Whitburn Colliery Railway.

The final L.M.S. Exhibit, No. 49, was a train of modern coaches built at the Derby Works of the former Midland Railway, hauled by No. 10474, a 4-6-0 of Lancashire & Yorkshire Railway design, one of 20 similar engines built at Horwich Works in 1924/5. A four-cylinder simple locomotive, No. 10474 was withdrawn in 1935, but the last survivor of the class remained in service until 1951.

The splendid Royal Train constructed by the Great Western Railway to mark Queen Victoria's Jubilee in 1897 appeared as Exhibit No. 50 behind locomotive 4082 "Windsor Castle".

Introduced in 1923, the "Castle Class" of the Great Western Railway were so successful that 171 were either built or reconstructed from older locomotives, the last being built as late as 1950. The first of the Class No. 4073 "Caerphilly Castle" is preserved at The Science Museum, London.

A second "Castle" class locomotive, No. 111 "Viscount Churchill" hauled a train of modern Great Western Railway coaches, built at Swindon and articulated in pairs on the system devised by Gresley. The locomotive is of particular interest, having started life in 1908 as the only 4-6-2 type locomotive ever built by the G.W.R. "The Great Bear". No. 111 was rebuilt as a "Castle" class 4-6-0 in 1924 and was scrapped in 1953.

The only Southern Railway exhibit in the procession was a modern train drawn by "King Arthur" Class 4-6-0 No. 449 "Sir Torre". Built at Eastleigh Works to the design of R. E. L. Maunsell in 1925, No. 449 was one of 74 Express locomotives bearing names associated with the Arthurian Legends. The class became extinct in 1962.

Contemporary travel on the East Coast Main Line was represented by a train of coaches built at York and Doncaster for the "Flying Scotsman" service. The locomotive, a majestic 4-6-2 (L.N.E.R. Class A2) No. 2400 "City of Newcastle" represented the final development of North Eastern Railway locomotive design, and was built at North Road Works in 1922. A further four engines were built, but they shared the fate of many small groups of non-standard locomotives and were scrapped, after comparatively short lives, in 1936/7.

Around the time that Exhibit No. 1 was passing the Grandstand, "The most brilliant spectacle of the whole wonderful parade . . ." as a reporter described it, was just running through Stockton, some six miles away. Ten chaldron wagons and a replica of the "coach" used by the S. & D. Committee on Opening Day, were filled with passengers in period costume, and the hundred year old "Locomotion", driven by a petrol engine concealed in a replica of the original tender, belched out smoke made by burning oily waste.

As the replica train rumbled towards Darlington, thousands of spectators flooded on to the line for a closer look, and many placed pennies, sixpences and even half-crowns on the rails to be flattened by the wheels of "Locomotion". Just before reaching the Grandstand, the spectacle was made even more realistic by a man carrying a red flag, and riding a large grey horse, at a safe distance ahead of the train, as was done at the Opening Ceremony in 1825.

In front of the Grandstand, the replica train clattered to a halt and "... the occupants fell forward in most amusing attitudes wildly clutching for some means of support . . . The Bandsmen (travelling in the two rear wagons) after sorting themselves out, collected enough breath to blow their instruments . . . and struck up 'Auld Lang Syne'. As they did so, the Duke and Duchess rose to their feet, and the men in the assembled throng bared their heads until the departure of the veteran engine."

THIS LOCOMOTIVE WAS BUILT BY
ROBERT STEPHENSON & Cº AT
FORTH ST WORKS NEWCASTLE-ON-
TYNE & WAS THE FIRST TO BE USED ON
A PUBLIC RAILWAY AT THE OPENING OF
THE STOCKTON & DARLINGTON RAILWAY
ON THE 27 SEP 1825. IT WAS DRIVEN BY
GEORGE STEPHENSON & HAULED A TRAIN
OF 90 TONS FROM SHILDON TO STOCKTON
A DISTANCE OF 18 MILES. IT CONTINUED
IN USE ON THIS LINE UNTIL 1841.

Reunited with its original tender, "Locomotion" on display at the Faverdale
Exhibition. The replica tender used in the Procession can be seen through the
door at the rear. The patchy look of "Locomotion's" chimney is apparently due
to the fact that ". . . souvenir hunters were content with a bit of tar from the
funnel". The Railway Centenary Celebrations were almost over, but there would
be one lasting benefit; the historic items at Faverdale were to form the
nucleus of York Railway Museum . . .

The L.N.E.R. issued a 74-page "Programme of Arrangements in Connection with the Railway Centenary Celebrations from Tuesday, 30 June to Wednesday, 8 July 1925" for use by members of the staff involved. This detailed document covered everything from train service alterations to arrangements for "conveyance of artistes luggage". The pages reproduced here deal with the movement of the Procession itself, and should be read in conjunction with the map on Page 8.

THURSDAY, 2nd JULY.

ORDER OF PROCESSION.

The procession will be composed of the following units. All engines, vehicles and trains forming the procession, except Nos. 47 and 54 will have been assembled previously on the Billingham Beck Branch.

These units will fall into the line of procession in their allotted places at North Shore Junction under the directions of the Stockton Yardmaster.

Each procession unit will carry a number tablet at the foot of the chimney for the purpose of identification.

The number tablets will be provided by the Chief Mechanical Engineer, who will arrange to place in position tablets for all units leaving the Works either at Darlington or Shildon.

Tablets for other L.N.E. units, except G.N. of S. Train No. 48, and for all the Foreign units, will be sent to the Yardmaster at Stockton, who will be responsible for placing them in position, either in the North Departure Sidings, or at North Shore Junction.

The tablet for the L.N.E. East Coast Train will be sent by the Yardmaster, Stockton, to the Yardmaster, Haverton Hill, and the latter will be responsible for having this placed in position.

The tablet for the G.N. of S. train will be sent to the Station Master, Newcastle, who will be responsible for having it placed in position.

The Chief Mechanical Engineer will send a representative to assist the Stockton Yardmaster to marshal and number the units.

A tail lamp will be carried only on the last vehicle of the last train in the procession, viz., "Replica Train."

Tablet Number.	Description.	Year Built.
	Freight Engines.	
1	Hetton Colliery Loco.	1822
2	The " Derwent "	1830
3	N.B. 0-6-0 J. 31 No. 1114	1867
4	No. 1275	1874
5	No. 517	1904
6	No. 934	1919
7	No. 203	1924
8	L.N.W. 0-8-0 4-cylinder No. 1881 ...	—
9	L.M.S. Heavy Freight No. 9446 ...	—
10	G.N. Mineral 2-8-0 No. 3499	—
11	G.W. 2-8-0 No. 4700	—
12	G.N. " Mikado " No. 2393	—
13	Shildon-Newport Electric No. 9 Mineral (Hauled by E.)	—
	Passenger Tender Engines.	
14	G.W. " North Star " on Crocodile ... (Hauled by E.)	—
15	" Cornwall," L.M.S.	1847
16	G.N. Single Driver No. 1	1870
17	Midland Single Driver No. 679	—
18	G.C. Single Driver No. 5972	1900
19	No. 910	1875
20	No. 1463	1885
21	No. 1620	1892
22	G.E. " Claud Hamilton " No. 8900 ...	1921
23	G.N. Atlantic No. 3990	1898
24	G.N. Atlantic No. 3251	1902
25	N.B. Atlantic No. 9902	—
26	No. 2207	1911
27	No. 2006	1899
28	G.C. " Lord Farringdon " No. 6169 ...	1917
29	L.N.W. " Sir Gilbert Claughton " No. 5900.	—
30	L.N.E. " William Whitelaw," No. 2563	1924
31	Cancelled.	
32	Electric Express Passenger (Hauled by E.)	—

Tank Engines.

33	Aerolite No. 66	1866	
34	G.C. Shunting Engine 407B, J. 61, No. 6499	1876	
35	G.E. Y. 6 No. 7133	1883	
36	No. 949	1874	
37	No. 1334	1894	
38	No. 2151	1913	
39	G.C. 4-6-2 No. 5088	1923	
40	L.M.S. " Baltic " No. 11112	—	
41	G.W. 2-8-0 No. 5225	—	
42	" Garratt " Locomotive	1925	
43	Petrol Bus 130	1922	
44	Petrol Autocar 2105	1923	
45	Sentinel Cammell Car	1925	

Trains.

46 T.3. No. 904, hauling L.N.E. Mineral Train of 10½, 20 and 40 ton mineral wagons, 30 wagons in all, 10 of each type, and 20-ton brake van.

47 T.1 No. 130, hauling L.N.E. Tableaux Train of six 40-ton quintuples and six 12-ton high goods wagons and van.

48 Engine 45A, hauling G.N. of S. Train of seven 4-wheeled coaches.

49 L.M.S. 4-6-0 No. 10474, hauling L.M.S. Corridor Train of nine vehicles.

50 G.W. " Windsor Castle," hauling G.W. Royal Train.

51 G.W. " Viscount Churchill," hauling G.W. Articulated Express Passenger Train.

52 Southern Railway Express Passenger Engine " Sir Torre " No. 449 and Modern Train.

53 L.N.E. " City of Newcastle," hauling East Coast Train.

54 " Locomotion," hauling Replica of Original Train.

No. 47.—Tableaux Train L. & N.E. Freight, six 40-ton Quintuples and six 12-ton high Goods wagons.

This train will be standing with engine attached at the south end of No. 3 Up Reception Line in Stockton Yard.

The train will convey Tableaux Artistes, and after they have taken their places on the train, a pilot engine will be attached in the rear and draw the train through No. 77 points on to the Up Main line, clear of the scissors crossing at North Shore Junction, the pilot engine being then detached. This train must then join in the procession in its proper place—see page 1146:

The signalman at North Shore Junction will be instructed by the Stockton Yardmaster when to alter the points to effect this movement.

The Yardmaster, Stockton, will arrange for a flagman on the Billingham Beck Branch to protect the Junction.

No. 48 unit will start from the Branch later to allow time for this movement.

The Tableaux Artistes must be in position at 10-15 a.m.

No. 53 L.N.E. EAST COAST TRAIN.

This train must stop at the Up platform in Stockton Station with engine cab opposite water column (a man with a white flag will be provided to mark the place) to pick up School Children, Boy Scouts and Girl Guides, Artistes' Baggage (see page 1152), Dining Car Attendants and Perishable Supplies.

The platform will be marked out for the various persons and commodities, in order that the loading up may take place as quickly as possible. The Station Master, Stockton, to arrange.

No. 54.—" Locomotion " and Replica Train.

This train will be standing in the North Shore Group of Sidings with " Locomotion " attached at the South End, and will convey Artistes and also one shunter on each Chaldron Wagon to apply the brakes if necessary. After these persons have joined the train, a pilot engine will be attached in the rear and draw the train back towards Stockton Bank on to the Down Independent, where pilot engine detaches. This train must then join in the procession in its proper place, through Nos. 81, 86 and 92 points.

The Yardmaster, Stockton, to see that this unit is provided with tail lamp, seeing it is the last train in the procession.

The Replica Train Artistes and Bandsmen must be in position at 10-30 a.m

INSTRUCTIONS TO TRAINMEN WORKING CENTENARY PROCESSION UNITS.

Trainmen will join the units to which they are allotted at the Haverton Hill end of the Billingham Beck Branch, at 7-30 a.m. on 2nd July.

At 8-0 a.m. the units will work forward slowly to the North Shore Junction end of the Branch. Each unit will wait until the preceding one has moved about 200 yards ahead before starting, and keep this distance until approaching the North Shore end, when they must close up and stand.

The route of the Procession will be as follows :—

On the Up Main Line from North Shore Junction to Hartburn Junction, thence through a facing temporary crossover road to the Down Line.

On the Down Main Line in the facing direction from Hartburn Junction to Eaglescliffe North, thence through No. 48 points from the Down Main to the Down Goods Line.

On the Down Goods Line in the facing direction from Eaglescliffe North to Eaglescliffe South, thence through No. 22 points to the Down Main Line.

On the Down Main Line in the facing direction from Eaglescliffe South to Oak Tree Junction.

On the Down Fighting Cocks Line in the facing direction from Oak Tree Junction to Fighting Cocks, thence through the existing crossover road to the Up Line.

On the Up Line from Fighting Cocks to S. & D. Crossing.

On the Down Independent from S. & D. Crossing to a point just ahead of the Water Column East of Albert Hill Junction, where the Down Independent will be slewed into the Up Independent.

Along the Up Independent and Up Reception Line in the facing direction past Albert Hill Junction box, continuing on the Up Independent in the facing direction to a point just short of Hopetown Junction, where the Up Independent will be slewed into the Down Independent.

On the Down Main Line from Hopetown Junction to Stooperdale signal-box, thence through the existing facing connection into Faverdale Works Sidings.

Pilotmen will not be provided for the facing line working on the route taken by the Procession units, and the leading driver of the Procession units when running in the facing direction will be given a hand-signal from each signal and gate box, as authority to proceed in accordance with General Rule 54.

The first unit of the Procession will leave North Shore Junction at 9-54 a.m., and the following units must draw forward so that they are ready at the North Shore Junction Home signal to take up their station in the Procession at the allotted interval. The Procession will travel at 6 miles per hour, and the leading unit will work to a definite Timetable, which will be in the hands of an Inspector on the first engine.

No. 53 "City of Newcastle" and East Coast Train will stop with the cab opposite the water column on Stockton Up Platform (where a man with a white flag will be stationed as marker) to pick up school children, etc.

No. 54 "Locomotion" and Replica Train will follow, and stand at Primrose Hill Signal-box until No. 53 proceeds.

These units must accelerate to 10 miles per hour after leaving Stockton until again in "Station."

The single units must "keep station" at intervals of 135 yards, and the trains at intervals of 270 yards. To enable this to be done, the line over which the Procession will pass is marked at 135 yards intervals by white boards in the 4-foot and on the parallel line by a whitened sleeper in line with the white board.

The second **single unit** must pass a white board as the leading unit clears the **next** white board ahead, and the succeeding single units must act in like manner.

The engines drawing **trains** must pass the white board in front of them as the unit ahead clears the **second** white board ahead, and so on.

At 6 m.p.h., 135 yards should be passed over in 46 seconds.

This time interval must be strictly adhered to by the driver of the first unit of the procession, and the other drivers must confine their attention to "keeping station" and obeying white flag signals and instructions from groundmen, where these are provided.

Enginemen must use their best endeavours to "keep station" without coming to a stand.

Should it be necessary, from any cause, for a unit to come to a stand, the fireman must hold out steadily, on the right-hand side of the footplate, a white flag, and the fireman on the following units must repeat this signal **at once** to the unit in the rear, which must immediately be brought to a stand and stop until the white flag ahead is withdrawn. When the flag is withdrawn, the units must **start** promptly.

The guards of **trains** must repeat the firemen's white flag to the train in the rear in each case, and a good look-out must be kept so that this can be done promptly.

The white flags for enginemen will be handed to each driver by the Chief Mechanical Engineer's representative. The flags for the guards will be handed to each man by the Stockton Yardmaster.

Should a unit break down and be unable to proceed without assistance, the fireman must at once go back, carrying the white flag steadily in his hand, to the unit in the rear, which must be drawn up to the broken-down unit, and then propel it throughout the Procession.

This arrangement must be carried out expeditiously, so as not to delay the Procession more than can be helped.

The units must then speed up to 10 miles per hour until they have again taken up their stations, care being taken to regulate the speed so that they can stop short of a unit ahead, should it come to a stand for any cause.

"Locomotion" and Replica Train must stop for exactly 2 minutes opposite the Grandstand and then proceed towards Fighting Cocks Station.

On approaching Fighting Cocks Station a good look-out must be kept for hand-signals.

Distribution of Processional Units at Fighting Cocks Station.

The head of the Procession will arrive at Fighting Cocks 11 22 a.m. :—

Units Nos. 1 to 45 both inclusive, must pass from the Down Facing to the Up Line through existing crossover at Fighting Cocks to closing up point at S. & D. Crossing.

No. 46. L.N.E. Mineral Train must pass through crossover to S. & D. Crossing, following units 1 to 45.

No. 47. L.N.E. Tableaux Train must pass through crossover and set back on Up Line to Fighting Cocks platform. After Artistes detrain the train will set back into Siding No. 26.

No. 48. G.N. of S. Train must continue on Down Facing Line towards S. & D. Crossing and come to a stand at "Limit" Board on North side of that line, 800 yards west of Fighting Cocks.

No. 49. L.M.S. Train must continue on Down Facing Line towards S. & D. Crossing, and close up to rear of No. 48.

No. 50. G.W. Royal Train must continue on Down Facing Line towards S. & D. Crossing, and close up to No. 49.

No. 51. G.W. Articulated Train must continue on Down Facing Line towards S. & D. Crossing, and close up to No. 50.

No. 52. Southern Railway Train must pass through crossover to proper Up Line, and proceed to closing up point.

No. 53. L.N.E. East Coast Train must pass through crossover road and set back to Fighting Cocks Platform.

No. 54. "Locomotion" and Replica Train must come to a stand on the Down Facing Line opposite the platform, and after discharging passengers proceed through crossover to Up Line. and then proceed to closing up point.

Movements to be made to remove Train Sets standing at Fighting Cocks Station.

(a) Engine " Viscount Churchill " detaches from G.W. Articulated Train and spare engine in Siding No. 1 pulls G.W. Articulated Train No. 51 back towards Fighting Cocks Bridge.

(b) Engine " Windsor Castle " to detach from G.W. Royal Train No. 50, and Engine " Viscount Churchill " attaches to G.W. Royal Train and draws it back on Down Line towards G.W. Articulated Train standing near Fighting Cocks Bridge, clear of connection leading from No. 1 Siding.

(c) Engine " Windsor Castle " then sets back into Siding No. 1.

(d) Engine " Viscount Churchill " backs Royal Train No. 50 along Facing Line to point clear of crossover.

(e) Engine " Windsor Castle " comes out of Siding No. 1, attaches to G.W. Articulated Train No. 51, spare engine having been detached, " Windsor Castle " draws train through crossover and proceeds towards S. & D. Crossing.

(f) Spare engine returns to No. 1 Siding, Royal Train drawn by " Viscount Churchill " is then allowed to proceed to Eaglescliffe where engine runs round and the train proceeds to York.

(g) L.M.S. No. 49 is then set back over crossover and proceeds to S. & D. Crossing.

(h) G.N. of S. No. 48 is then set back over crossover and proceeds to S. & D. Crossing.

(i) As soon as L.N.E. East Coast Train is ready to return to Eaglescliffe and Stockton it must be drawn forward towards S. & D. Crossing clear of crossover, where engine " City of Newcastle " will be detached. Spare engine from No. 1 Siding will then attach to train and leave for Eaglescliffe and Stockton at 2-30 p.m. Engine " City of Newcastle " to be put inside at Fighting Cocks until return of East Coast Train at 3-35 p.m., when spare engine is detached and " City of Newcastle " works train to S. & D. Crossing on proper line.

(j) Tableaux Train stationed in Siding No. 26 will proceed towards S. & D. Crossing as soon as L.N.E. Train has left for Eaglescliffe and Stockton, and engine " City of Newcastle " has been disposed of.

Movements to be made between S. & D. Crossing and Faverdale Works Sidings.

As the units approach S. & D. Crossing, they will close up as before-mentioned, and will be worked across the Main Line into Faverdale Works in the following manner :—

Each unit will be worked forward to the water column at Albert Hill, where it can take water, if necessary.

Units must not remain stationary on Skerne Bridge (No. 21), and must pass over it one at a time.

From the water column the units must proceed singly towards Hopetown Junction at speeds not exceeding 10 miles per hour, and close up.

From Hopetown Junction the single units will be worked forward in batches into Faverdale Works.

Guard Woodhouse will travel on the last unit of each batch from Hopetown Junction Box into Faverdale Works Sidings.

Mineral Train No. 46 and Tableaux Train No. 47 will proceed from Hopetown Junction to Shildon Sidings.

The G.N. of S. engine (Unit No. 48) will detach the seven 4-wheeled coaches at Charity Junction, proceeding thence to Faverdale Works, via Stooperdale Curve, and be placed in the Exhibition Sidings.

L.M.S. No. 49; G.W. "Windsor Castle" and Articulated Express Passenger Train, No. 51, and Southern Railway Train, No. 52; L.N.E. "City of Newcastle" and East Coast Train No. 53, and "Locomotion" and Replica Train, No. 54, will proceed into Faverdale Works.

The line between S. & D. Crossing box and Hopetown Junction box will be reserved exclusively for the Procession units, which will follow one another as directed.

All drivers must be prepared to receive hand-signals from groundmen throughout the movements detailed above.

Inspectors will be in charge at S. & D. Crossing box, Albert Hill water column, Hopetown Junction, and at the entrance to Faverdale Works. At Stooperdale Box a pilotman will be provided to conduct the units into Faverdale Works Sidings.

A Supply train, with water tanks and hand-pumps, will be working on the Down Line between S. & D. Crossing box and the "Limit" board, situate 800 yards west of Fighting Cocks, to supply any engines which have run short.

Trainmen.

As the procession units may be delayed in getting over S. & D. Crossing and into Faverdale Works Sidings, arrangements must be made if necessary to relieve trainmen.

Trainmen—continued.

Trainmen who are lodging at Haverton Hill will return there, either **by** ordinary or special train, after the units are all housed in the Exhibition Sidings.

The ordinary train service from Darlington Bank Top to Haverton Hill in the afternoon is as follows :—

	p.m.	p.m.		p.m.	p.m.		p.m.	
Darlington, Bank T. dep.	3 55	5 4		6 37	9 9		10 40	
Eaglescliffe arr.	4 11	5 20	}	6 53	9 25	}	10 56	} change
dep.	4 20	5 31	}	7 11	9 34	}	11 5	}
Stockton ...arr.	—	5 37	} change	—	—		11 11	
,, ...dep.	—	5 42	}	—	—		—	
Billingham arr.	4 49	5 54		7 31	9 54	} change	—	
,, dep.	5 5	6 5		7 36	10 0	}	—	
Haverton H.arr.	5 9	6 9		7 40	10 4		—	

If trainmen have not been able to travel by the last ordinary train on 2nd July, they must travel by Guest Specials, which leave

Faverdale at 10-15 or 10-43 p.m.

Bank Top at 10-53 p.m.

Stockton arrive at 11-16 p.m.

and a charabanc will be available at Stockton to take passengers to Haverton Hill. Or, if the trainmen are later than this, a special must be run from North Road Station to Stockton. The District Superintendent, Darlington, to arrange and advise the Station Master, Stockton, before 10-0 p.m. if a charabanc is required, and at what time.

Drivers of all units between Stockton and Faverdale must keep a sharp look out for trespassers, and sound their whistles as may be necessary.

The success of the Procession will largely depend upon the successful maintenance of a uniform speed of 6 miles per hour, and the accuracy with which the units " keep station," and drivers are requested to pay particular attention to these two points.

Acknowledgements

All photographs published in this book are from original prints taken during the 1925 Centenary Celebrations with the exception of "Henry Oakley".

Issued under the auspices of C. W. F. Cook, Public Relations Officer, British Rail, Eastern Region, York.

Production and Design by Ronald H. Deaton, Public Relations Department, British Rail, Eastern Region, York.

Production assistance by British Transport Films Photographers, York.

Captions by Stuart L. Rankin, Public Relations Department, Eastern Region, York.

Complete the Trilogy

If you have not yet got your copies of the forerunners to this book — "Cavalcade Reflections" and "Cavalcade Retrospect" which recorded the 1975 Cavalcade — supplies are still available at 65p per copy including postage and packing (U.K. only) from: Public Relations Officer, British Rail, Eastern Region, West Offices, York YO1 1HT.

Bonus Offer

And for £1 including postage and packing (U.K. only), you can secure, from the same address, your own copy of the full 30 — page Special Trains Notice which governed all movements at the Cavalcade.